Melodramatic Muse

AF624483

Alyssa Thomson

BookLeaf
Publishing

Presentation by *BookLeaf Publishing*

Web: www.bookleafpub.com

E-mail: info@bookleafpub.com

ISBN: 978-93-95969-45-1

First edition 2022

DEDICATION

To everyone that has supported and kept my passion for writing alive,

this book would not exist without you.

PREFACE

Growing up, I've come across my fair share of people that thrive off of misery. More specifically, the misery of others to mask the misery within themselves. They collectively brought me down to my lowest low. Throughout this book, I've shared my deeply personal thoughts while navigating through times of uncertainty. It is so easy to forget that words have a dual meaning of power. Words can drag you down in the blink of an eye, or they can help you rise to the top and make you stronger. Only you can decide that power. Here, I've decided on mine.

Greetings

Corpse hands and a glistening grin

black roses in hands covered in lace ever so thin

eyes darker than the depths of the seas,

feet breaking after each step

this is how I choose to greet death.

The Bright Side

The heavens, the skies, the fates all know

we cannot live a fulfilling life all on our own.

To love and care,

to hold and share.

A love without life may be so,
but a life without love is no way to go.

Run away from it all and you miss out,

Making memories and prancing about.

Dancing and singing to the stars above,

Surrounded by friends and family you love.

The love, the laughs and the tears all combined,

keeps the cycle of life completely aligned.

A reason for everything is sure to be true,

Everyone would miss you and the world would be blue.

Take each day and make it better than the last,

Do the best that you can, any dread will surely pass.

You are strong,

Stronger than you know,

Every step you take is sure to glow.

A step is a step no matter how small,

You will one day rise to ten feet tall.

Go live the life you want to live.

Not for anybody.

anybody except

for you.

Glass Heart

To love and be loved;

nothing more, nothing less.

Ten years young with her glass heart broken-

broken by the one with words left unspoken.

She cries into the void with no one around.

No one around to hear her excruciating sounds.

False hopes and false promises were everything he ever said-

Not before long he left her on read.

The months and the years flew by like stormy winds at sea,

nothing ever changed, nor did he.

She knew better to just let it be.

Through the agony and tears she grew thick skin,

it was never her fault, nothing she ever did.

Your absence spoke louder than her voice could cry

without any care she left with a wordless goodbye.

Bitter

Even if I could,

trust me I would

turn back time to before we met,

for I would rather

endure a thousand cuts

and a lifetime of pain

than to have you back in my life

for just

one

second.

Different

Her eyes a forest, an evergreen glow

Cheeks raised a permanent grin

Hair dark as night with skin white as snow

Confidence radiating, barely wearing thin.

To the world she may seem small

beaming with light she's brighter than the sun

She barely stands just over five feet tall.

Yellow and golden, all around fun.

No jewel in the world could compare

A caterpillar to some

To the ones she owns, filled with so much care

For the girl I speak, she is me

For this is all I could ever be.

Acting

I made my bed

I dug my grave

I knew the consequences

I did it all anyway.

For what purpose

did any of that possess?

An actor,

I guess I may be.

Does anybody know

the real side of me?

Artist

There's something beautiful in every day,

Through pictures and words I express

The world around, inspiring in some way

Adding colours to my canvas hoping to de-stress.

Each day a new start

Vibrant fiery reds mixed with cool calming blues

Flowers and petals blossom all through my art.

How can I stop creating when I have so many hues?

Palette harmony is what I aim to achieve

Telling a thousand words with no words at all

Each piece has meaning waiting for you to perceive

An artist I am, this is my call.

Life through colour and words within,

Life through an artist, I've a permanent grin.

Runaway

Wouldn't it be fun?

To pack it all up and run

thousands of miles

just you and me

with the hope to find

a place by the sea

Live new,

let go.

A fresh start away from this deadbeat town

we've only ever called home.

No more tears,

No more fears.

Pack it all up for the unknown,

it's time to find ourselves

a brand new place

for us to call home.

Second

Second thought

second best.

Always the bridesmaid,

never the bride.

Too young to die,

nothing to die for.

No direction,

just a mess.

Don't do this,

Don't do that.

When will it matter,

Will it be so hard to accept

that I'm not okay

and none of this

is the best.

Is there truth to the madness?

or am I just depressed

Belong

I found where I belong

Somewhere along the way

through the pleasure

through the pain

talking with you about the rain

hands in mine

kisses so sweet

I was always certain

you belong with me.

Aimless

Maybe

Just maybe,

I'm floating aimlessly

Doing just enough to get by

not enough to soar.

Motionless it seems

navigating reality

to an unknown future.

What am I to do?

Helium won't last forever.

Neither will I.

How long is it

until my balloon pops

with not even myself

to float from

the demons

that keep

dragging.

Me.

Down.

Slither

Snake skin hands

with words like venom

rolling off your tongue

second-hand lover,

are you sure

they're the one?

Free

The heaviest weight

I have lifted

was the misery

the abuse,

and everything about you

to finally be

the master of my own fate

for now I am free

fully able

to be me.

Quarantine

Will everything be okay

if we carry on each day

the same as the last

never much change

with our homes a prison

there is not much we can do

only wander and weep between these walls

not really living,
just existing

completely bound by the laws

hands tied behind our backs

longing to be free

with no more fear

and a true will

to live again.

Questions

Who am I?

Who are you?

Who's to say we are or aren't

If everything is real or fake

Who's truth is true

Who's lies are lies

Does anybody care

What else is out there

Beyond our reach

And through the stars

Maybe we need to know

What we don't know and accept

That is true

Unless we don't exist at all

All these cries go unheard

From a being barely 5 feet tall.

Little Love

Little one filled with so much life

May all your dreams be filled with eternal
happiness,

that smile of yours be ever-growing,

and your mind

believing all that you can and all that you will,

my little love.

I'll hold your hand dear to mine

never will I ever

leave

your

side.

Nothing Lasts Forever

White picket fence and an ocean view

All that's missing

is no longer you,

rather the faint sounds of a heartbeat

other than my own,

fading into nothing

completely

utterly

alone.

Alone, I was

before I met you

I thought I knew

what it meant to be alone.

You changed my mind in many ways

the sun seemed so much brighter day after day

we built this home,

so we could be

no longer

alone.

Here I stand,

on the porch in front of the white picket house

saddened by the knowledge

of how a house is only a house

until you make it a home.

How can I call it a home

when dust continues to pile

over your side of the room

perfectly un-perfect,

exactly the way it was left

that fateful day

we had to lay you to rest.

Rough waves engulf the shore

too far away to extinguish the pain

of the entire house consumed by flames

a single tear made its way to the floor

for nothing is left to make memories anymore.

Goodbye,

My love.

And to

my once

perfect

home.

Narcissist

For I have tried

no less than a thousand times,

to get you to see

what life is like on my side

only to find you staring

at none other than yourself.

Lies flood behind your eyes

false tears and false promises-

It was all the same to you.

You played me as a game,

cheated your way through,

did you have your cake

And eat it too?

Saviour

You cannot help someone

that does not want to be helped.

No matter how much

you bend over backwards,

push your limits beyond the edge,

they will not listen to you.

For their mind is made

not for you to disrupt.

They're playing their cards

the only way

they know how.

You know what that is like

You know how hard it is to float

having inner demons

slither around you

wasting no time

constricting

to the point of suffocation

beyond repair

Every.

Single.

Day.

You will shatter yourself,

your whole existence in pieces

trying to make sure

no one else has to endure

every one of their demons

completely on their own.

You can't be their saviour.

They are the only one

who can truly

save

themselves.

Crush

How lame must it be

to bite my tongue

until it bleeds,

holding back the words

and the courage

to confess

every single thing

I've been holding back

letting you live rent free in my mind

I wish I was

always by your side.

Forward

Some things are better

better off unknown,

Save your heart.

save your ache.

For the tears and the pain

are barely worth

knowing what you already knew.

Carry on, darling.

Don't ever look back.

Turn the page, a new chapter awaits.

www.ingramcontent.com/pod-product-compliance
Lightning Source LLC
Chambersburg PA
CBHW051750130826
49812CB00033B/1090
* 9 7 8 9 3 9 5 9 6 9 4 5 1 *